YO-AGU-167

BOILING WATER IN A PAPER CUP

•

AND OTHER UNBELIEVABLES

JEROME S. MEYER

SCHOLASTIC BOOK SERVICES

NEW YORK • TORONTO • LONDON • AUCKLAND • SYDNEY • TOKYO

This book is sold subject to the condition that it shall not be resold, lent, or otherwise circulated in any binding or cover other than that in which it is published—unless prior written permission has been obtained from the publisher—and without a similar condition, including this condition, being imposed on the subsequent purchaser.

Copyright © 1970 by Scholastic Magazines, Inc. All rights reserved. Published by Scholastic Book Services, a division of Scholastic Magazines, Inc.

3rd printing . . . . March 1974
Printed in the U.S.A.

A Collection of Curiosities,
Incredible Statements as well as
Amazing Facts that seem Impossible
until You read the Explanations
at the End of the Book
Profusely Illustrated with
Drawings and Diagrams by
William Hunter

Cover Design by Bill Pesce

1. BOILING WATER TILL IT FREEZES

Everyone knows that water boils at 212 degrees Fahrenheit. Unless you have studied physics, you won't know that the boiling point is lowered as the atmospheric pressure is decreased. So the statement that water boils at 212 degrees Fahrenheit is not accurate unless the pressure of the atmosphere is specified. At sea level it is 760 millimeters, and if this normal pressure is reduced as little as seventeen millimeters, the water will boil at about 180 degrees Fahrenheit. People who live on mountains, where the atmospheric pressure is much less than it is at sea level, find water quite easy to boil — but difficult to get to the temperature we all call "boiling hot."

It is obvious that if the pressure of the air is constantly decreased, the boiling point will be lowered and will in time reach 32 degrees Fahrenheit, or the freezing point. By electrically heating a pot of water, enclosing it in an airtight jar, and gradually pumping all of the air out of the jar, the boiling point of the water can be made as low as the freezing point and the boiling water will start to freeze.

The apparatus for this experiment is very complicated; nevertheless it demonstrates that boiling water will turn to ice when the air pressure is sufficiently low.

2. SEE? — NO HANDS!

Glue a small, thin piece of cardboard to the bottom of an empty spool, and make a hole in the cardboard so you can blow clear through the spool. Now hold a playing card against the cardboard, as shown, and stick a pin through the card so that it projects up into the hole of the spool. If you let go, of course the card will fall off; but if you blow very hard into the spool, you will find that you can remove your hand and the card will still cling to the spool. You can't blow the card away! How do you explain this?

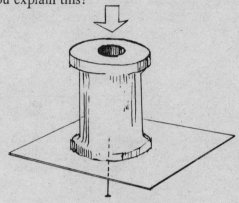

3. AMAZING COLOR WHEEL

Here you see a black and white wheel — no color anywhere. But watch what happens when you spin it. To do this, cut out

the wheel, mount it on cardboard, and put a pin through the center. Spin it clockwise, and the outside ring will turn *blue,* the middle one *green,* and the inside one *red!* Spin it counter-clockwise, and the colors will be reversed. How's that for an unbelievable? If you're mystified, consult the Answer Section.

4. MYSTERY MAN

He is quoted daily by millions — more than any other man living or dead — yet almost no one knows him by name. Do you?

5. GOING TWO WAYS AT ONCE

It seems unbelievable that a train moving forward has backward motion at the same time. How do you explain this phenomenon?

6. THE FLEXIBLE NINES

Eleven can be written with three nines, thus:

$$\frac{99}{9}$$

In that case, how would you write twenty with only three nines?

7. SOME PILE!

Suppose it were possible to cut a large sheet of paper in half, then in quarters, eighths, sixteenths, and so on for fifty-three cuttings. If you then piled up all the strips of paper, one on top of the other, how high would the pile be?

8. DOUBLING BY HALVING

Sound impossible? Well, here's how it's done: Cut a thin strip of paper about fifteen inches long and an inch wide. Fold the strip over on itself and paste the ends together, as shown in the diagram. Now take a pair of scissors and cut down the middle of the strip, beginning at any point and cutting all around. When you have finished cutting, you will find that instead of two rings of equal size, as you would expect to get, you have a ring *twice as large* as the original one.

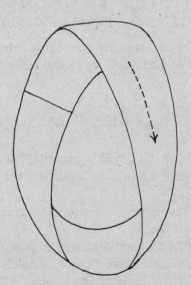

9. NO REPEATING DIGITS

Long words that have no repeating letters are rare. Here are a few: *playground, dumbwaiter, workmanship, republican, sympathizer*. Even more difficult to find are eight-digit numbers in which no digits are repeated. Four such numbers are:

58132764   72645831   76125483   81274365

Note that the digit 9 is missing from each of these numbers.

Still more unusual is the fact that if you multiply any of the numbers by 9 and 18, the results are a nine- and ten-digit number in which no digit is repeated:

$$58132764 \times 9 = 523194876$$
$$72645831 \times 9 = 653812479$$
$$76125483 \times 9 = 685129347$$
$$81274365 \times 9 = 731469285$$
$$58132764 \times 18 = 1046389752$$
$$72645831 \times 18 = 1307624958$$
$$76125483 \times 18 = 1370258694$$
$$81274365 \times 18 = 1462938570$$

As far as we know, there are no other numbers that behave in this way. But go ahead and try to find some if you have the urge!

10. GUESS WHAT?

Can you guess what this object is from the following clues?

• It is not a solid, a liquid, or a gas, not animal, vegetable, or mineral.

• It is constantly moving and can reproduce itself, yet it is not alive and never was.

• It is extremely common and very important to all of us. Give up? The answer is unbelievably simple.

11. A BILLION — MORE OR LESS

a. Suppose you wanted to count from one to a billion by tapping out the numbers on a table. Assuming you're now sixteen years old and that you tap away day and night, without interruption, at the rate of one number every second — or sixty taps a minute — how old would you be before you finished counting?

b. Suppose you have a billion dollars and invested it in a company run so badly that it lost a thousand dollars of your investment every day of the week — including Sundays. How long would it be before your money was all gone?

12. HYDROSTATIC PARADOX

The diagram shows two vessels, A and B, each filled with water to the same level. The area of the base is the same for each vessel, although B holds a hundred times as much water as A. Which sustains the greater pressure on its base, A or B?

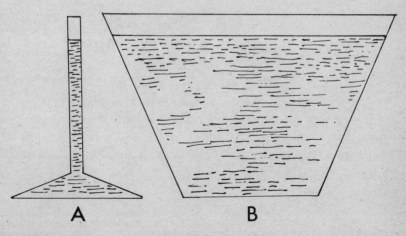

A   B

13. FLYING IN REVERSE

Birds always appear to fly forward. This means that if they want to reverse direction, they have to swerve around in an arc, thereby wasting a lot of time. In this respect a man driving his car has the advantage over a flying bird, because he can back up and reverse direction without going through a U-turn. There is one bird, however, that by changing the slant of its feathers can actually fly backward. It is the hummingbird — the only creature in all birddom than can do so.

14. YOU'RE SEEING THINGS

You may think you're reading the type on this page, or any other page, but as a matter of fact you're doing no such thing. What you actually see is the white paper surrounding the black type, and the type is a silhouette. Black is the total absence of color or reflected light — in other words, total darkness, which can't be seen.

15. PASSING A SOLID THROUGH AN IRON GRILLE

On the face of it, this would seem an impossible feat. Yet there is a sure way to accomplish it. On a grille of very fine steel wires, place a hundred-pound cake of ice. The ice will actually force its way through the grille, and in an hour or two will be *under* it instead of over it.

16. INCREDIBLE BUT TRUE

Did you know that you can hold a glassful of water, covered with a thin piece of cardboard, upside down without spilling any of the water or causing the cardboard to fall off? The diagram shows how. Try it and see for yourself. Be sure the glass is full, and experiment over a basin first. How do you explain this feat?

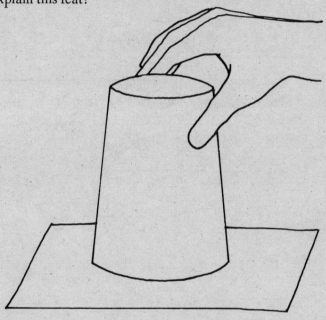

17. THE LARGEST THREE-DIGIT NUMBER

Offhand you probably would say that 999 is the largest number with three digits, but this is not so. The largest three-digit number is $9^{9^{9}}$. This represents 9 multiplied by itself 387,420, 498 times. Written in numerals this size, this number would stretch from New York to Chicago. To read it would take more than a week. Nobody knows what the number is, but some mathematicians claim that it begins with 428 and ends with 89. This number is more than 100 billion times the number of electrons in the entire universe!

18. GYROGEOMETRY

Here's one you should be able to figure out in seconds. The diagram shows a circle with radius of 8.2 feet. If BC is 4.5 feet, how long is AB?

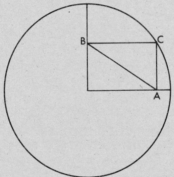

19. THE DISAPPEARING DOLLAR

This is not a new problem, but it's very interesting nevertheless. Three men registered at a hotel and asked for separate rooms. They were assigned three rooms at ten dollars apiece, and paid the clerk a total of thirty dollars. The next day it was discovered that the men had been overcharged — the total room rent should have been twenty-five instead of thirty dollars. A bellboy was instructed to return the difference of five dollars to the men. But the boy, being less honest than he might have been, decided to give each man back *one dollar* and keep *two dollars* for himself. This meant that each man was paying *nine dollars* for his room — or a total of *twenty-seven dollars* for the three rooms. But $27 + 2 = 29$. Where did the other dollar go?

20. CANNON-BALL CONUNDRUM

Two cannon balls, identical in size and weight, are taken to the top of a tower two hundred and fifty feet high. The first ball is shot from a cannon at the very instant that the second ball is dropped. The first ball travels two miles, while the second ball travels only two hundred and fifty feet — yet they both hit the ground at the same time. How can that be?

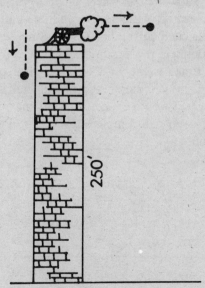

21. THE LONGEST PAINTING

John Banvard, the painter, decided to paint a panorama of the Mississippi River, from its source in Lake Itasca, northern Minnesota, to the city of New Orleans — a distance of 2,348 miles. It took over a year and a little more than *three miles of canvas* to complete the painting, which was then wound on two metal drums similar to the reels of a movie camera.

Banvard first exhibited his remarkable creation in Louisville, Kentucky. For two hours, observers watched spellbound as the panorama unfolded. It was like sitting on the deck of a Mississippi riverboat and watching the scenery go by.

22. REVOLUTIONARY PROBLEM

The diagram shows a big wheel on the ground, and a little wheel on an elevated platform two-and-one-half feet above the ground but fastened to the big wheel. Since its radius is five feet, in one complete revolution the big wheel travels ahead on the track ten times π feet, or 31.41 feet. Yet so does the little wheel although its circumference is only half that of the big wheel, so that you would expect it to advance only half as far — 15.70 feet — in one complete revolution. Puzzled? See the Answer Section.

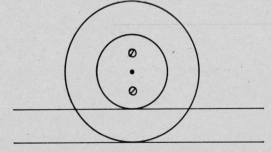

23. FOUR-IN-ONE

"Last night," said Julian, "I dined with my grandfather, my stepbrother's nephew's father, my father's mother-in-law's husband, and my stepmother's father-in-law — yet I dined alone. Unbelievable? Maybe — but Julian told the truth.

24. MYSTERIOUS TRIANGLE

Figure A shows an equilateral triangle, each side two inches long. Figure B results from cutting two of the sides in half and projecting them down to the base, so that we now have two equilateral triangles, each with sides of one inch instead of two inches. Figure C repeats the same process as before, so we now have four triangles of the same base, each with one-half-inch sides.

You can see that we can keep on doing this indefinitely without changing the original perimeter, which happens to be six inches. So it would seem that the area of the original triangle will ultimately vanish, though the perimeter always remains the same. How do you explain this?

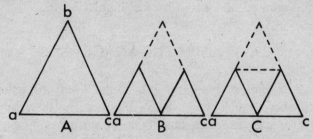

25. SHAKE A LEG — IF YOU CAN

Would you believe it possible to stand on both feet and yet not be able to move one leg in any direction? Here's how it's

done: stand sideways against a wall, so that all of one side —
from shoulder to foot — is touching the wall. Now try to move
the outside leg. It can't be done.

26. A TWELVE-STORY WAVE

On August 27, 1883, the volcanic island of Krakatoa — between Java and Sumatra in the South Pacific — exploded,
sending millions of tons of dust twenty miles into the air,
destroying more than three hundred villages, and killing about
thirty-six thousand people. Heard on the island of Rodriguez
three thousand miles away, the explosion created great air
waves that circled the globe seven times, affecting barometers
everywhere. Dust from Krakatoa settled in every part of the
world for weeks after the explosion. This island of eighteen
square miles, with an elevation of fourteen hundred feet above
sea level, was blown to pieces, leaving in its place a huge sea-
bottom cavity a thousand feet below the surface. The explosion
had the intensity of twenty-five of the largest hydrogen bombs,
and the tidal wave resulting from it formed a vertical wall of
water a hundred and thirty-five feet high!

27. ENIGMATIC ANAGRAMS

Most of us think of anagrams as a game played with letters of
the alphabet, to make new words out of old. But there is much
more to a true anagram than that. In a true anagram, you
rearrange all the letters in a group of words or sentence to form
another group of words or sentence having a definite relation
to the first. For example, *the eyes* becomes *they see; there
we sat* becomes *sweetheart.* Bearing in mind this principle,
consider these two remakable anagrams:

He saw his ragged Continentals row.

becomes:

Washington crossing the Delaware.

To a merry Christmas and prosperous New Year.

becomes:

Happy days return; no more scares or war times.

Check both of these anagrams, letter by letter, and you will see that all of the original letters have been used.

28. FIVE DAYS IN SPACE

On June 14, 1963, the Russian astronaut, Lieutenant Colonel Valery F. Bykovsky, started to orbit the earth. On June 19 — five days later — he had completed eighty-one orbits and covered more than two-million miles. In that period he saw the sun rise and set eighty times, and crossed the 180th meridian as many times. Since it is well known that you gain or lose a whole day each time you cross this meridian, it would seem that in crossing it eighty times the astronaut should have gained or lost nearly three months. Yet when he returned to earth, only five days had passed. What's your explanation?

29. SOMETHING TO EXCLAIM ABOUT

Punctuation is as important in mathematics as it is in English composition. For example, it makes a big difference where you put a comma (to indicate thousands) or a period (decimal point). Similarly, the use of an exclamation mark after a number radically alters its meaning (magnitude). Let us say you are asked how many one-fourth-inch squares there are in a rectangle whose sides are respectively one and one-and-a-quarter inches. Your answer should be 20. But if you were to add an exclamation — 20! — you would be saying 2,432, 902, 008,176,640,000 squares! That number of one-fourth-inch squares would more than cover the entire United States. How can a mere exclamation mark make such a big difference?

30. ALWAYS ROOM FOR ONE MORE

Who says no two bodies can occupy the same place at the same time? The following experiment would seem to disprove this universal law. Fill a glass to the brim with water, and drop in pins (or one-inch nails), one at a time. You will find that you can drop up to a couple of hundred pins into the glass without causing any overflow. And apparently the process can go on almost indefinitely. How do you explain it?

31. SUPERMAGIC SQUARES

a. IXOHOXI. Everyone knows that in a magic square all rows and columns, and the two diagonals, always add up to the same number. In the square shown below, all rows and columns add up to 19,998 — even if you turn the figure upside down. But that is not all: if you look at it in a mirror, where everything is reversed, you will find that all rows and columns still add up to 19,9998! The name IXOHOXI has been given to this remarkable square because it reads the same forward, backward, upside down, and in the mirror.

8818	1111	8188	1881
8181	1888	8811	1118
1811	8118	1181	8888
1188	8881	1818	8111

b. Forcing Squares. By definition, the true magic square not only must add up to the same sum along the rows, files, and long diagonals, it must also use a number only once, and use only numbers that form a consecutive series — like 2, 3, 4, 5 etc. So the IXOHOXI square is not quite perfect, for it utilizes nonconsecutive numbers.

Well, here is a square with consecutive numbers used once each. But its rows, files and long diagonals do not add up to the same sum, so it is far from a proper magic square. Nevertheless, it has a peculiar magic of its own. With it, you can announce a certain sum in advance — then "force" people to name that very sum!

1	2	3	4	5
6	7	8	9	10
11	12	13	14	15
16	17	18	19	20
21	22	23	24	25

Start by asking someone to circle a number with a pencil. Then have him cross out the numbers of the same horizontal row and vertical file as the circled number. Next, tell him to circle any other number not crossed out, then cross out the numbers in the same row and file as the second circled number. Have him repeat the procedure two more times, which will leave one number. He should circle it.

Add up the circled numbers, and the sum will always be 65. Try it!

To make sure you know how to work this unbelievable little stunt, take a look at the following example:

• Say 4 is picked first and the numbers in its row and file crossed out. Then the square would look like this —

1	2	3	(4)	5
6	7	8	9	10
11	12	13	14	15
16	17	18	19	20
21	22	23	24	25

• Say 15 is picked second and the numbers in its row and file crossed out. Then the square would look like this —

1	2	3	4	5
6	7	8	9	10
11	12	13	14	(15)
16	17	18	19	20
21	22	23	24	25

• Say 17 is picked third and the numbers in its row and file crossed out. Then the square would look like this —

1	2	3	4	5
6	7	8	9	10
11	12	13	14	(15)
16	(17)	18	19	20
21	22	23	24	25

• Say 8 is picked fourth and the numbers in its row and file crossed out. Then the square would look like this —

1	2	3	4	5
6	7	(8)	9	10
11	12	13	14	(15)
16	(17)	18	19	20
21	22	23	24	25

• Only 21 remains. Circle 21. Add up all the circled numbers: $4 + 8 + 15 + 17 + 21 = 65$.

You can work the trick, if you prefer, with squares of more rows or fewer rows. Just remember to number the places in the square consecutively, thus:

1	2	3	4	5	6	7
8	9	10	11	12	13	14
15	16	17	18	19	20	21
22	23	24	25	26	27	28
29	30	31	32	33	34	35
36	37	38	39	40	41	42
43	44	45	46	47	48	49

(Forces 175)

1	2	3	4
5	6	7	8
9	10	11	12
13	14	15	16

(Forces 34)

32. PROVING THE IMPOSSIBLE

Here is "proof" that a right angle is greater than 90 degrees:

Given rectangle ABCD, with all four angles right angles. Using D as center and DB as radius, draw DB′ so that angle B′DC is greater than 90 degrees. Now join A and B, and erect perpendicular bisectors on AB and AB′. Since these two lines are neither parallel nor coincident, the two perpendiculars will meet at some point, here shown as O. Now join AO, CO, DO, and B′O.

22

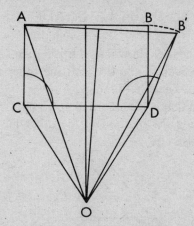

Triangles ACO and B'DO are congruent, because the three sides of one are equal to the three sides of the other:

AO = B'O (on the perpendicular bisector of AB')
OC = OD (on the perpendicular bisector of CD)
AC = B'D (equal to BD, which is also equal to AC)

Therefore angle ACO is equal to angle B'DO (same parts of congruent triangles). But angle DCO equals angle CDO (base angles of the isosceles triangle OCD). Hence angle ACD equals angle B'DC, or a right angle is equal to an angle greater than 90 degrees.

Unbelievable? Of course it is. Can you find the mistake?

33. BOILING WATER IN A PAPER CUP

Did you know that you can place a paper drinking cup on the stove and light the burner under it without burning the cup at all? Of course, you first have to fill the cup with water. If you do that, and keep the flame fairly low, the cup will not catch fire. The water will even boil in the cup! How come?

34. DIGITAL DEADLOCK

Place your hands as shown in the diagram. Notice that the fourth fingers touch at the tips and the other fingers (all but the thumbs) are knuckle to knuckle.

You will find that you cannot separate your two fourth fingers without changing the position of the other fingers.

Frustrating, isn't it?

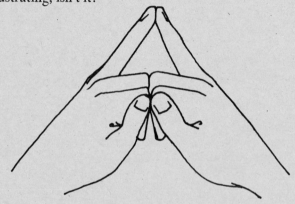

35. HOW HEAVY IS HEAVY?

We think of a heavy object as one hard to lift. But weight, or heaviness, is a relative concept, and things heavy on earth may be light on other planets — and vice versa. For example, you would find it easy to lift a cubic inch of even the heaviest earth metals, like lead or osmium. On the other hand, a cubic inch of dust from the star Sirius, also known as the Dog Star — a dwarf star in the constellation Canis Major — would weigh a ton on earth! Just a few grains of this star dust in your salt shaker would cause the table on which the shaker stands to collapse, and probably also the floor under it. A suitcase full would weigh more than eight locomotives. So the next time you complain of something being heavy, just think of Sirius!

36. STICK 'EM UP WITHOUT STICKUM

It's a fact! You can actually place playing cards on a wall and have them stay there without using any kind of adhesive — paste, glue, rubber cement, gummed tape — or other fastener. If you want to know how, turn to the Answer Section.

37. SLIPPING A QUARTER THROUGH A DIME-SIZED HOLE

Skeptical? Well, here's how it's done. Put a dime in the center of a piece of paper and trace around it with a pencil. Then fold the paper straight through the center of the penciled circle, and cut around the tracing to make a dime-sized hole. Next, holding the paper as shown, place a quarter over the hole and bend up the folded sides of the paper. Now slip the quarter through the hole without tearing the paper!

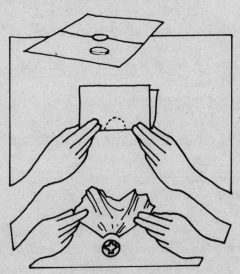

38. EVERY TRIANGLE IS ISOSCELES

Draw any triangle ABC, as shown. Draw a perpendicular bisector MN on base AB. Now draw OD and OE perpendicular to AC and CB, respectively. Join AO and BO.

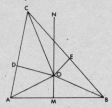

We will now prove that triangle ABC is isosceles.

Angle DCO = angle OCE (we made them equal, since C is bisected).

The angles at D and E are right angles, and side CO is common to both triangles. Therefore CD = CE (same parts of congruent triangles).

Since O is on the perpendicular bisector of AB, OA = OB.

Since triangles COD and COE are congruent, DO = OE.

But AO = OB. Therefore triangles AOD and EOB are congruent (two sides and an angle are equal) and AD = EB (same parts of congruent triangles).

But we have proved that DC = CE and AD = EB. Therefore AC = CB and triangle ABC is isosceles.

What's wrong with this proof?

39. GETTING OVER THE HUMP

Suppose a very thin metal pipe one mile long were placed on flat ground. Suppose it were possible to push the ends of the pipe together one foot, so that the pipe would rise toward the middle and leave only 5,279 feet between the ends of the pipe still on the ground. The question now is, how high would the hump be? One foot? Five feet? Ten feet?

26

40. MONKEY BUSINESS

The illustration shows a little monkey on a string that goes around a pulley and has a weight on the other end of it. The weight and the monkey are exactly the same — they balance each other — so if the monkey remains still, nothing happens. But suppose the little fellow starts to climb the rope, will the weight go up or down on the other side?

41. NOW YOU SEE IT — NOW YOU DON'T

Who says that fresh, clean water is always transparent? Just fill an ordinary clear glass with running water and place a coin behind it, as shown here. Now look at the coin from the top of the glass, viewing it through the surface of the water and through the other side of the glass. Bet you can no longer see the coin clearly. What seems to be the problem?

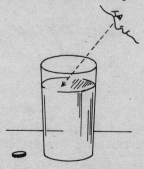

42. THREE QUERIES

a. The picture shows a man standing on the beach, facing the horizon. In the distance is a tiny ship, A. Far to the north of A is another ship, B. If ship A is fifteen miles from shore, how far away is ship B?

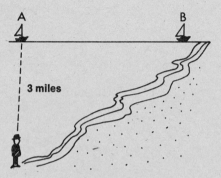

b. Two poles, A and B, each six feet high, are standing upright on the ground on a bright, sunny day. The distance between the poles is four feet, and the time is 3:00. Pole A casts a four-foot shadow, while pole B's shadow is twelve feet long. How do you account for this difference?

c. All printed matter is reversed in a mirror. Can you arrange two mirrors in such a way that the print will *not* be reversed?

43. MY GRANDSON IS OLDER THAN I AM

My grandson has just turned 100 years old. I have hopes that in 1,010 years he will be entering high school, and that by the time he is 10,101 he will be finishing college. How can this be?

44. REMARKABLE REVERSALS

In each of the following groups of figures, there is an interesting relation between those on the left and those on the right. If you study them closely, you will see how truly remarkable these reversals are.

$$9 + 9 = 18 \qquad 9 \times 9 = 81$$
$$24 + 3 = 27 \qquad 24 \times 3 = 72$$
$$47 + 2 = 49 \qquad 47 \times 2 = 94$$
$$497 + 2 = 499 \qquad 497 \times 2 = 994$$

$$21^2 = 441 \qquad 12^2 = 144$$
$$31^2 = 961 \qquad 13^2 = 169$$
$$201^2 = 40401 \qquad 102^2 = 10404$$
$$211^2 = 44521 \qquad 112^2 = 12544$$

45. WHEN IS WATER NOT WET?

When it is dry. And that is no joke. Just add two teaspoonsful of zinc stearate to a glass of water and let it float on the surface. Now dip the tip of your finger — not more than an inch — into the water. When you take it out, you will find that your finger is perfectly dry! Try it and see for yourself.

46. PRAISE BEE!

The bee is truly an amazing creature. It has five eyes and five thousand nostrils. Its wings vibrate at the rate of 11,400 times a minute, and its sting is the result of coordinate action by twenty-two muscles. In order to gather one pound of honey, a bee must travel a distance equivalent to twice around the earth!

The wasp, though structurally less complicated than its cousin the bee, has played a vital role in the history of our civilization. It is from the wasp that man learned the secret of making paper from wood pulp. The wasp chews up wood and plant fibers, making a powder and mixing it with an adhesive substance produced in its own body. The result is a fine pulp that the insect eventually transforms into many layers of paper in a remarkable manner. The paper product, dark gray in color, is of exceptionally good quality — light in texture, yet quite tough as well as water-resistant. Today, 90 per cent of our paper is made from logs — thanks to the example of the wasp!

47. STRAIGHT-LINE MAGIC

It's hard to believe that the beautiful and intricate geometric designs shown here have been created with straight lines only.

Unconvinced? Use a magnifying glass and see for yourself — not a curve in sight! Why not try making some straight-line magic of your own?

48. TRISECTING AN ANGLE WITH RULER AND COMPASS

This has been called an impossible feat, like squaring a circle. Actually, there's nothing easier than trisecting an angle with ruler and compass — provided you don't use an *unmarked* straightedge. Here's how it's done:

Given angle ø to trisect. With C as center, draw any semicircle cutting the base line. With a straightedge, mark off the radius of the semicircle, calling this distance AB. Now lay the straightedge in such a manner that it touches D, the point at which the semicircle and the side of angle ø intersect, with point B touching the semicircle and point A on the base line. You have now formed angle o, which is exactly one third as large as angle ø.

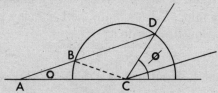

In case you have any doubts about the validity of this procedure, see the Answer Section.

49. THE CRESCENT AND THE CROSS

This is a very tricky task, but you can do it if you put your mind to it. You are to divide the crescent shown here into six parts that will fit neatly in the cross above it. Hint: one of the parts has to be reversed. Check your results with the diagram in the Answer Section.

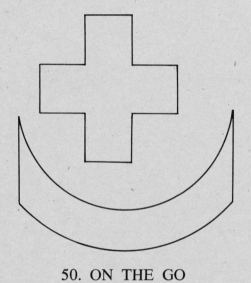

50. ON THE GO

Joe Doaks travels more than twenty-five miles every day except Sunday, without ever using any form of transportation — car, bus, train, plane, boat, or horse — and without either walking or running. What's more, he has many people traveling with him. How does he do it?

51. ARITHMETICAL COINCIDENCES

It would seem from the following examples that multiplication and division are the same as addition and subtraction. Can you think of other "coincidences" like these?

$$1\frac{1}{2} \times 3 \text{ or } 1\frac{1}{2} + 3 = 4\frac{1}{2}$$

$$1\frac{1}{3} \times 4 \text{ or } 1\frac{1}{3} + 4 = 5\frac{1}{3}$$

$$1\frac{1}{4} \times 5 \text{ or } 1\frac{1}{4} + 5 = 6\frac{1}{4}$$

etc.

$$1 \times \frac{1}{2} \text{ or } 1 - \frac{1}{2} = \frac{1}{2}$$

$$2 \times \frac{2}{3} \text{ or } 2 - \frac{2}{3} = 1\frac{1}{3}$$

$$3 \times \frac{3}{4} \text{ or } 3 - \frac{3}{4} = 2\frac{1}{4}$$

etc.

$$1\frac{1}{3} \div \frac{2}{3} \text{ or } 1\frac{1}{3} + \frac{2}{3} = 2$$

$$2\frac{1}{4} \div \frac{3}{4} \text{ or } 2\frac{1}{4} + \frac{3}{4} = 3$$

$$3\frac{1}{5} \div \frac{4}{5} \text{ or } 3\frac{1}{5} + \frac{4}{5} = 4$$

etc.

$$4\frac{1}{2} \div 3 \text{ or } 4\frac{1}{2} - 3 = 1\frac{1}{2}$$

$$5\frac{1}{3} \div 4 \text{ or } 5\frac{1}{3} - 4 = 1\frac{1}{3}$$

$$6\frac{1}{4} \div 5 \text{ or } 6\frac{1}{4} - 5 = 1\frac{1}{4}$$

52. MUSIC KNOWS NO BOUNDS

The International Opera House in Rock Island, Quebec, is uniquely situated on the U.S.-Canadian border. During a performance, the audience is in America while the actors are in Canada!

53. FALL SAFE

Do you know that you can jump off the roof of the tallest building in the world — the Empire State Building in New York City — and yet not be seriously injured when you hit the ground? If you don't believe it, see the Answer Section.

54. AN ARM EQUALS A FOOT

Strange as it may seem, your forearm — from elbow to wrist — is the same length as your foot. Measure them and see for yourself.

55. NOT A SHADE OF DIFFERENCE

Two airplanes, identical in size and wingspread, are flying over the field at noon on a bright sunny day. The first plane is only fifty feet above the ground, while the second is five hundred feet up. You would expect the shadow cast by the plane that is nearer the ground to be larger than the shadow cast by the plane that is farther away. Actually, however, both shadows appear the same size. How do you account for this?

56. MAGNETIC HILL

A few miles out of Moncton, Canada, on Route 33, the curious Magnetic Hill remains at odds with the law of gravity. Here's what happens if you drive to the foot of the hill, put your car in neutral, and shut off the gas: your car begins to *coast uphill*, gathering momentum as it goes! How can this be?

57. AN ALL-TIME RECORD

Very often in our reading we come across a sentence that could easily be shortened and would be the clearer for it. Too long a sentence tends to confuse and bore the reader. Yet in what is probably the longest sentence ever written, Victor Hugo, in *Les Miserables,* packs a masterful characterization of the French king Louis-Philippe into a mere 823 words — helpfully punctuated with eighty-nine commas, fifty-one semicolons, and four dashes — and manages to hold our interest to the end! Here it is:

Son of a father to whom history will certainly grant extenuating circumstances, but as worthy of esteem as his father was of blame; possessing all the private virtues and several of the public virtues; careful of his health, his fortune, his person, and his business affairs; knowing the value of a minute, but not always the value of a year; sober, serious, peaceful, and patient; a good man and a good prince; sleeping with his wife, and having in his palace lackeys whose business it was to show the conjugal couch to the citizens — a regular ostentation which had grown useful after the old illegitimate displays of the elder branch; acquainted with all the languages of Europe, and, what is rarer still, with all the languages of all the interests, and speaking them; an admirable representative of the "middle classes," but surpassing them, and in every way greater;

possessing the excellent sense, while appreciating the blood from which he sprang, of claiming merit for his personal value, and very particular on the question of his race by declaring himself an Orleans and not a Bourbon; a thorough first prince of the blood, so long as he had only been Most Serene Highness, but a frank bourgeois on the day when he became His Majesty; diffuse in public and concise in private life; branded as a miser, but not proved to be one; in reality, one of those saving men who are easily prodigal to satisfy their caprices or their duty; well read and caring but little for literature; a gentleman, but not a cavalier; simple, calm, and strong; adored by his family and his household; a seductive speaker, a statesman who had lost his illusions, cold-hearted, swayed by the immediate interest, governing from hand to mouth; incapable of rancor and of gratitude; pitilessly employing superiorities upon mediocrities, and clever in confounding by parliamentary majorities those mysterious unanimities which growl hoarsely beneath thrones; expansive, at times imprudent in his expansiveness, but displaying marvelous skill in his imprudence; fertile in expedients, faces, and masks; terrifying France by Europe, and Europe by France; loving his country undeniably, but preferring his family; valuing domination more than authority, and authority more than dignity; a temperament which has this mournful feature about it, that by turning everything to success it admits of craft and does not absolutely repudiate baseness, but at the same time has this advantage, that it preserves politics from violent shocks, the state from fractures, and society from catastrophes; minute, correct, vigilant, attentive, sagacious, and indefatigable; contradicting himself at times, and belying himself; bold against Austria at Ancoma, obstinate against England in Spain, bombarding Antwerp and paying Pritchard; singing "La Marseillaise" with conviction; inaccessible to despondency, to fatigue, to a taste for the beautiful and ideal, to rash generosity, to utopias, chimeras, anger, vanity, and fear; possessing every form of personal bravery; a general at Valmy, a private at Jemappes, eight times attacked by regicides, and always smiling; brave as a grenadier and courageous as a thinker; merely anxious about the chances of European convulsion, and unfitted for great political adventures; ever ready to risk his life, but not his work; disguising his will in influence for the sake of being obeyed as an intellect rather than as king; gifted with observation and not with divination; paying but slight attention to minds, but a good judge of man — that is to say, requiring to see ere he could judge; endowed with prompt and penetrating sense, practical wisdom, fluent tongue, and a prodigious memory, and incessantly drawing on that memory, his sole similitude with Caesar, Alexander, and Napoleon; knowing facts, details, dates, and proper names, but ignorant of the various passions and tendencies of the crowd, the internal aspirations, and concealed agitation of minds — in one word, of all that may be called the invisible currents of consciences; accepted by the surface, but agreeing little with the lower strata of French society; getting out of scrapes by skill; governing too much and not reigning sufficiently; his own Prime Minister; excellent in the art of setting up the littleness of realities as an obstacle to the immensity of ideas; mingling with a true creative faculty of civilization, order, and organization, I do not know what pettifogging temper and chicanery; the founder of a family and at the same time its man-of-law; having something of Charlemagne and something of an attorney in him; but on the whole, as a lofty and original figure, as a prince who managed to acquire power in spite of the jealousy of Europe — Louis-Philippe would be ranked among the eminent men of his age, and among the most illustrious governors known in history, if he had loved glory a little, and had a feeling for what is grand to the same extent that he had a feeling for what is useful.

58. EGG IN A BOTTLE

Without cracking the shell, you can get an egg into a bottle whose opening is smaller than the diameter of the egg. Take an empty milk bottle — a wax carton won't do — insert a burning piece of paper, and place the egg in the bottle opening. The flame will burn out the air in the bottle, causing the pressure from above to push the egg right into the bottle. Try it and see.

59. DOUBLE DILEMMA

A certain king, who had two sons, left this unusual will:

Upon my death, my sons shall ride straightway to the neighboring city of Blenheim. To the one who gets there last, I bequeath my entire kingdom.

Accordingly, when their father died, his sons mounted their horses and headed for Blenheim — a distance of two hundred kilometers. But since each was determined to get there last, they soon reached a point where neither would move a step ahead of the other. Finally, as they stood next to each other on the highway, hopelessly deadlocked and at a loss as to what to do, they met a man who offered a solution. Can you guess what it was?

60. CALLING ALL COMMAS!

Punctuate these sentences so that they make sense:

1. Not and I said but or.
2. That that is is that that is not is not.
3. Whereas in the quiz Jones had had had Smith had had had had. Had had had had the examiner's approval Smith would have passed.

61. WORD LORE

a. Every word in the English language is supposed to have at least one vowel, and most words of five or more letters contain at least two vowels. Here are some unusual combinations:

- A five-letter word with four vowels: *queue*.
- A nine-letter word with only one vowel: *strengths*.
- An eleven-letter word containing all five vowels in order: *facetiously*.
- A legitimate word with no vowels at all: *cwm* — pronounced koom and meaning "valley." Note that in order to be able to pronounce it, the letter *w* is given the sound of a vowel.

b. Words of twenty or more letters are a rarity, although they can be found in the dictionary. Most people think that the longest word in the English language is *antidisestablishmentarianism,* with twenty-eight letters. But there is another legitimate word which holds the record with forty letters: *pneumonoultramicroscopicsilicovolcanokoniosis* (a disease of the lungs).

Chemistry claims big words, too. As far as we know, the longest one has fifty letters: *paraminobenzoyldiaethylaminoethanolumphydrochloricum.*

Your dictionary will help you break these mouthfuls into bite-size syllables so that you can pronounce them.

62. TWO-TIME LOSERS

Here are two "knotticisms" that stump even the experts:

1. *A barber shaves everyone in town who does not shave himself.* Now the question is: does the barber shave himself?

If he does, he is breaking the rule by shaving someone who shaves himself. But if he does not, he is breaking the rule by failing to shave someone who does not shave himself.

2. *Lawyers never tell the truth. I am a lawyer.* According to this statement, if I am a lawyer, I am not telling the truth: therefore I am *not* a lawyer. Conversely, if I am not a lawyer, I am telling the truth: therefore I *am* a lawyer.

63. HOW GOOD IS YOUR EYESIGHT?

Here are a few eye-foolers which disprove the old saying that "seeing is believing." To find out whether your eyes have deceived you, check your answers to the following statements by means of ruler and compass.

a. Which wall is nearer the staircase, A or B? Look at the diagram from all angles.

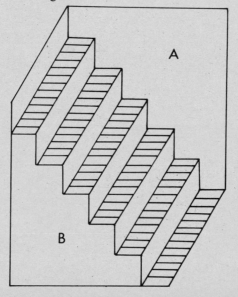

b. Is *Figure A* higher than it is wide? Is *Figure B* wider than it is high?

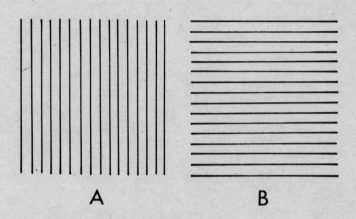

A   B

c. Vertical lines *A, B, C, D,* and *E* are not parallel.

A B C D E

d. Which is longer, A or B?

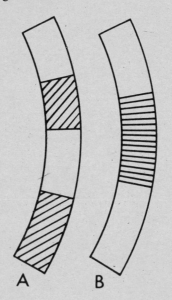

e. Are lines A and B straight? Are they parallel?

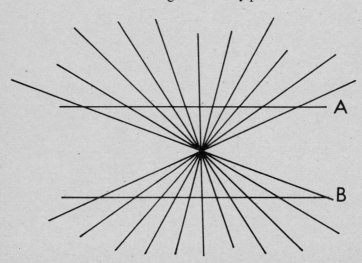

f. Which is longer, AB or CD?

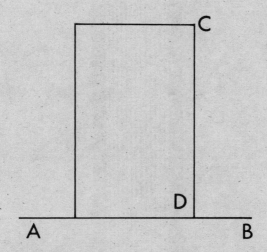

g. Which is smaller, arc A or arc B?

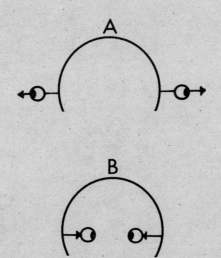

h. Which is the continuous straight line, B C or AC?

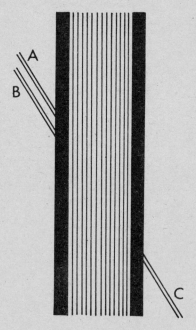

i. The white spaces separating *A, B,* and *C* vary in width, do they not?

j. Which is longer, AB or BC?

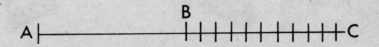

k. Diagonal lines A, B, C, D, E, F, G, and H are not parallel — or are they?

l. Which is the greater distance, from A to B or B to C?

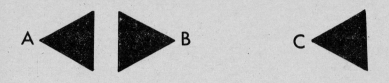

64. FUN WITH FIGURES

a. You would expect to get the same answer if you multiplied two fractions together or their equivalent decimals. Then how do you account for the different answers in this example?

$$16 \frac{1}{2}$$
$$\times \quad 12 \frac{1}{2}$$
$$\overline{\quad 32 \quad}$$
$$16$$
$$8 \frac{1}{4}$$
$$6 \frac{1}{4}$$
$$\overline{206 \frac{1}{2}}$$

$$\times \quad \frac{16.5}{12.5}$$
$$\overline{825}$$
$$330$$
$$165$$
$$\overline{206.25}$$

Which is the right answer?

b. Here's proof that $1 = 2$:
Let $a = b$. Then:

$$ab = b^2$$
$$ab - a^2 = b^2 - a^2$$
$$\text{and } a(b - a) = (b + a)(b - a)$$

46

Dividing out b — a, we get:
$$a = b + a$$
$$\text{or } 1 = 2$$

What's wrong with this reasoning?

c. Joan is 4,380 times as old as John, who is twice as old as Jane. They all have the same mother, who is twenty times as old as Joan. If the ages all add up to a little over twenty-one years, how old is each child?

d. Here's a memory trick sure to impress your friends — until they catch on. Hand out the following list of numbers, noting that each is composed of ten digits:

1.	3145943707	*5.*	7189763921
2.	4156178538	*6.*	8190998752
3.	5167303369	*7.*	9101123583
4.	6178538190	*8.*	0224606628

Now ask a friend to pick any one of these ten-place numbers, identifying it by the number in italics at the left. Then state that you will reel off the corresponding ten-place number *from memory!* Here's the way you fake it.

Suppose your friend picks number 3: 5167303369. Then all you do is to add 12 to 3 mentally, getting 15; then reverse the digits to get 51 — which of course is the beginning of that number series. Now just keep adding the last digit to the one before it *eight times,* and you'll have the whole series of digits in their correct order. Thus:

$5 + 1 = 6, 6 + 1 = 7, 7 + 6 = 13$ (use only the 3),
$3 + 7 = 10$ (use only the 0), $0 + 3 = 3, 3 + 0 = 3,$
$3 + 3 = 6, 6 + 3 = 9$

It's easy when you get the hang of it. But don't forget to stop after naming the ten digits.

65. THE FORCEFUL FINGER

Tell a friend to grip an ordinary wooden pencil by its two ends and hold it up, then confidently boast that you can break it with just one finger. He will not believe you.

So make a fist and raise it high, poking out your forefinger as if you are about to ram it down on the pencil. Instead, as you swing, hit the pencil with your fist, at the same time keeping your forefinger extended. Your fist will break the pencil in two — but it will look exactly as if your finger did it!

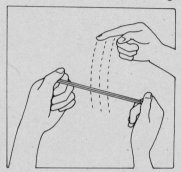

One warning. The trick may not work if the pencil is shorter than, say, 6 inches.

66. UNBELIEVABLE GEOGRAPHY

A fugitive from justice is being pursued by police but steps across the line into another state where they have no jurisdiction. The fugitive then recalls that the police of this second state, too, are after him. So he takes one step, thus escaping to a third state. He suddenly recalls, however, that the police of the third state want him also. Therefore he takes one more step and finds himself in a fourth state, where he is safe.

Unfortunately for him, that last step was so hurried that he tripped. Part of his body fell into the state from which he had first escaped — whereupon the police arrested him.

Where could such a scene take place?

67. SHORTHAND — OR IS IT LONGHAND?

a. If you know how, you can write down 100 by using all the numbers from 1 to 9, using them once only, and using no other numbers.

b. You can also write down 100 by using six 9's only. In the same way, you can write down 89 by using six 8's only and 78 by using six 7's only.

Don't believe it? Turn to the Answer Section.

68. GUESSING THREE CARDS

Discard from a deck all cards of 7 or higher. This leaves you with the twenty-four lowest cards, ranging from ace to 6. Turn your back and ask someone to choose three cards from the twenty-four, laying out the three left to right. Suppose his choice is as shown below. Ask him to do the following mental arithmetic:

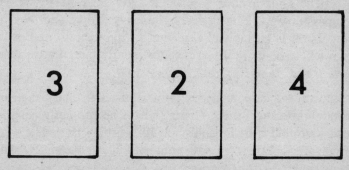

Double the value of the first card (=6).
Add 5 (=11).
Multiply by 5 (=55).
Add the value of the second card (=57).
Multiply by 10 (=570).
Add the value of the third card (=574) *and tell you his result.*

No matter what that result, you subtract 250 from it and the answer will always reveal the cards he chose. Thus, 574 — 250 = 324.

69. GEOGRAPHY JAMBOREE

Like a sense of humor, a sense of direction is something everyone prides himself on. This quiz assesses your sense of direction, and also your knowledge of geography. If you get every item right without peeking at a map, it will be more than unbelievable. It will be a miracle!

a. An aviator bound for London leaves New York City and heads due east. After crossing the Atlantic he finds himself not over London but over Madrid. What's wrong with his compass?

b. The same aviator is scheduled to return via Rome. His compass now working perfectly, he leaves Rome and flies due west. He figures this will take him to the vicinity of Boston, from where he can turn in a southwesterly direction to reach New York City. Is he right?

c. A ship's captain heads through the Panama Canal and emerges into the Pacific Ocean, where he promptly runs his vessel aground to avoid collision with a fishing boat. The ship's owner, who wants an explanation, lives in Pittsburgh. By radio he directs the captain to fly up by the shortest route. The captain charters a plane, has the pilot fly approximately northeast. The pilot decides the captain's brains must have been addled by the shipwreck. Why?

d. If on the whole you agree with any of the following statements, mark it T. If on the whole you disagree, mark it F.

1. Los Angeles lies more to the west than to the east of Reno. . . .
2. Death Valley lies more to the north than to the south of Los Angeles. . . .
3. Texas is the largest state. . . .
4. No state touches four Great Lakes. . . .
5. Chicago lies more to the east than to the west of New Orleans. . . .
6. Detroit lies more to the east than to the west of Atlanta. . . .
7. Salt Lake City lies more to the north than to the south of Indianapolis. . . .
8. Denver lies more to the north than to the south of Washington, D.C. . . .
9. Montreal lies more to the south than to the north of Seattle. . . .
10. Houston lies more to the west than to the east of Kansas City. . . .
11. New York City lies more to the north than to the south of Barcelona. . . .
12. Montreal lies more to the north than to the south of Paris. . . .
13. New York lies more to the north than to the south of Istanbul. . . .
14. Cape Horn lies more to the west than to the east of Montreal. . . .
15. Saigon lies more to the south than to the north of Mexico City. . . .
16. Miami lies more to the west than to the east of Havana. . . .

17. London lies more to the north than to the south of Quebec. . . .

18. The Cape of Good Hope lies more to the north than to the south of Cape Horn. . . .

70. INFLATION OR DEFLATION

It cannot be denied that 25 cents = $\frac{1}{4}$ dollar.

Square roots of equals are equal. So the square root of 25 = the square root of $\frac{1}{4}$ dollar.

Therefore 5, the square root of 25 = $\frac{1}{2}$, the square root of $\frac{1}{4}$.

In other words, 5 cents = $\frac{1}{2}$ dollar.

Anything wrong?

71. PUZZLE OF THE POOL

Deciding to build a swimming pool, Mrs. Manybucks hired an architect and a plumber. She told them to make sure it could be quickly filled after being emptied for cleaning. So the architect recommended filling through a 3-inch pipe at the shallow end and a 3-inch pipe at the deep end. The plumber bitingly remarked that a single 6-inch pipe would fill the pool faster. The architect retorted that a 6-inch pipe would be slower. A heated discussion followed.

Annoyed, Mr. Manybucks came out of the house. Calling the two men incompetent, he ordered them off the job. Any fool, he shouted, would know that a pair of pipes each 3 inches in diameter was the equivalent of one pipe 6 inches in diameter.

Who was right — the architect, the plumber, or Mr. Many-bucks?

72. TWO SHAPES FOR ONE

Get yourself a sheet of graph paper. Out of it cut a square like the one shown here. Then cut the square into three pieces that can be combined to make both of the forms below.

You don't believe it can be done? Try it, anyway. Maybe you'll surprise yourself.

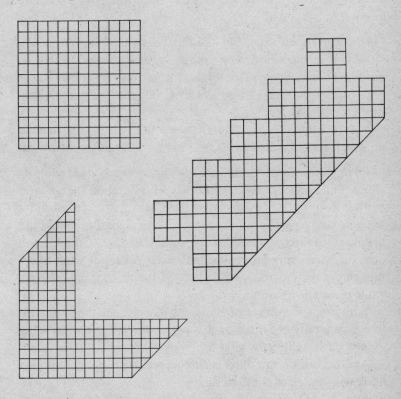

73. WONDERS OF THE WILD

• Did you know that the largest snakes in the world are the pythons slithering through East Indian jungles? Their cousins, the boas of South America, sometimes approach 30 feet in length but pythons occasionally exceed 30 feet.

The largest poisonous snake in the world is the king cobra of southeastern Asia, and its venom is the deadliest. It reaches lengths of 15 feet and more.

Like the rattlesnake, which can go without food for a year, the python may fast many months at a time. But when he does eat, his appetite is prodigious. He can swallow a goat whole and digest it horns and all.

• Here's an unbelievable. Mount Everest is not the tallest mountain in the world! Oh, it's the highest, all right. That is, its 29,141-foot peak is the highest point on the globe. But it rises from a plateau 15,000 feet high. Therefore the mountain proper is 14,141 feet high.

Mount McKinley, in Alaska, beats that. From the plateau on which it stands, it rises 14,500 feet to its 20,300-foot crown.

• The cormorant, fishing underwater, propels itself with its wings. Penguins also swim with their wings, but on the surface. In that fashion, it is said, they tirelessly cover scores of miles without stopping. Antarctic penguins, incidentally, surely are the most devoted parents in the bird kingdom. Couples will take turns carrying an egg on their feet to keep it from freezing, one penguin going without food for as long as 60 days while the other is foraging.

While on the subject of birds, let us consider the swan. He is not generally regarded as a superior flier. Yet he can wing along comfortably at a solid 50 miles per hour.

Another interesting bird is the parrot. He uses his bill as a hook with which to climb trees.

• Think a firefly is something special because it can flash a light for a second or two? In the tropical Americas one species of beetle carries around two globes on its neck that it can keep lit for minutes at a time. Headlights?

• The oldest trees? In Australia there are stands of Macrozamia that include specimens some 15,000 years old. The oldest animals? Giant tortoises — especially the Galapagos variety, which can live two centuries. The oldest man? At this writing it is Shirali Mislimov of Azerbaijan, Soviet Union, reported by *The N.Y. Times* to be 163 years old.

74. BY SPECIAL ARRANGEMENT

Sam was about to leave on his summer vacation. He wanted to take along his favorite old fishing pole, a one-piece monstrosity of bamboo 7 feet long. But the bus line would not accept luggage more than 6½ feet long.

Unbelievably, Sam fixed it so that the bus driver could load the pole into the baggage compartment without breaking the rules. How did Sam do it?

75. UNBELIEVABLY TRIANGULAR

With five straight lines you can draw ten triangles. Five of the triangles overlap — and that's a clue.

76. DRAMA IN ANCIENT ROME

Young Cassius, a student, hands an arithmetic example to Brutus, the teacher. It looks like this:

$$XI + I = X$$

Of course, Brutus says Cassius is wrong and flunks the poor fellow. Cassius may be wrong, but is Brutus right?

77. EDUCATED PLAYING CARDS

Take any one suit out of an ordinary deck of playing cards and eliminate the 10, jack, queen, and king. With the nine remaining cards you can pull some cute tricks.

• First, tell somebody to pull out any three cards while your back is turned and lay them on the table so as to form a number. Suppose the cards are:

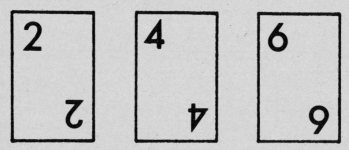

Now tell him to take the rest of the deck and with cards from it form the reverse of the original number. Tell him to subtract the lower number from the higher, setting out his answer with still other cards. His layout will then look like this:

Finally, ask him to name the card at the right of his answer. It's a 6, he says. You immediately proclaim that the other cards are 3 and 9.

How do you do it? Well, the middle card will always be 9. And the sum of the answer cards will always be 18. Subtract 9 and 6 from 18, and you get the third card, a 3.

• Dare somebody to set up the nine cards so that they add up to 100. Unbelievable, maybe — but it can be done three ways:

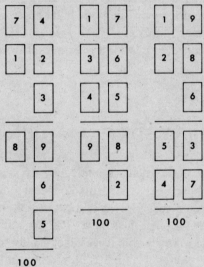

• Inform a friend that you can lay out the nine cards, plus others from the deck, to demonstrate that 45 can be subtracted from 45 and still leave 45. When he scoffs, arrange the cards this way:

9	8	7	6	5	4	3	2	1	= 45
− 1	2	3	4	5	6	7	8	9	= 45
8	6	4	1	9	7	5	3	2	= 45

78. GUESSING ODD OR EVEN

Sue Smart had an argument with Gilbert Goof and Billy Blowhard. They boasted boys had better heads for figures than girls, but Sue disagreed. To prove her point, she asked that one pick an odd number and the other an even number — and not tell her what the numbers were or who had picked which.

Sue directed Gilbert to double his number and Billy to triple his, then add the results. When they gave their answer, she promptly announced which boy had chosen an odd number and which an even number!

Sue's trick dates back at least to Shakespeare's day. Can you figure it out?

79. HOW FOXY CAN YOU GET?

Farmer Brown had 5 fields bounded by 16 fences, as shown in the drawing. A fox, leaving his den near one of the fields, was spotted by Farmer Brown and promptly chased. The fox fled, crossing each fence just once. This so confused the good farmer that the fox was able to get back safely to his den.

Are you as foxy as the fox? With a continuous line starting and ending at the den, cross each fence only once.

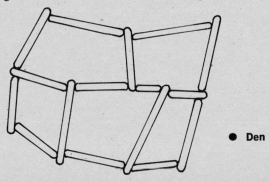

● Den

80. LOST BUT NOT LEAST

Here is the most puzzling, exasperating, mystifying, unbelievable puzzle in this book or perhaps any other book. It's all the more unbelievable because no trickery is involved. It happens right before your eyes!

It starts with the problem of dividing this rectangle into four parts that can be recombined to form a square:

Only three straight lines may be used to divide up the rectangle. That may make the problem a bit difficult, so we'll solve it for you:

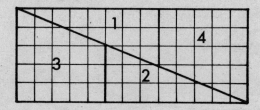

Identifying each of the four parts by a number, we combine them to make this square, as you see.

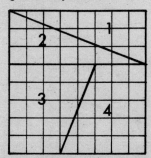

So far, so good. The problem is solved. But now comes the mystery. Count the small squares in the original rectangle. They number exactly 65. Now count the small squares in the square. They number 64. Yet the square contains all the parts of the rectangle.

How is that possible? What happened to the missing small square? *It seems to have vanished into thin air!*

That disappearing act has tantalized youngsters and oldsters, philosophers and dunces, magicians and mathematicians, for hundreds of years. It is the biggest little unbelievable of them all.

81. UNTYING A KNOT IN HUMAN HAIR

Offer to bet that you can undo a knotted hair. If anybody takes you up on it, you can't lose. Unbelievable? Well, here's how to manage it.

1. Pluck a hair out of your head, or anybody else's head, and tie a simple knot as shown.

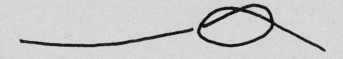

2. Draw the knot as tight as possible without snapping the hair. It will then be almost invisible and cannot be untied with the fingers — even with the aid of tweezers, pins, or other tools.

3. Place the hair in the topmost crease of your palm, the knot near the palm's edge and the tail of the knot protruding. Liberally moisten the knot with saliva.

4. Close your fist, and start pounding the tail against your other palm, as shown.

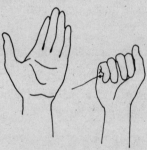

5. It will take a few minutes but if you keep pounding, the knot will begin to open up. Continue to pound. Soon the knot will be sufficiently loosened for you to untie it with your fingers.

82. BE RIGHT EVERY TIME

Here's an unbelievable little trick that makes you seem a mind-reader. Ask someone to choose any number but not tell you what it is. Have him add 7 to the number and double that sum, then add 3 and multiply by 5.

Now request his answer. From it subtract 85, then divide by 10. Your result will always be the number he chose!

83. FREAKS OF PHYSICS

• Suppose you have a full glass of water. A couple of lumps of ice are floating on the water, sticking up higher than the rim. But when the ice melts, the water will not spill over.

• Salt is used to freeze ice cream. It is also used to melt ice.

• Every liquid, as it loses heat, contracts. But water, as it loses heat — as it freezes, that is — will burst a pipe.

• Thick, heavy cream will float on thin milk, even on skim milk.

• A gallon of water and a gallon of alcohol, if mixed, will make less than two gallons of liquid.

• Take a cupful of the water and pour it into the alcohol. Take a cupful of the resultant mixture and pour it back into the water. There will then be as much water in the alcohol as there is alcohol in the water. For explanations, see Answer Section.

84. ASK MOTHER NATURE

Sometimes life takes such strange forms, and survives in such odd ways, that the mind cannot credit them. Who would conceive, for example, of the sloth, an animal that eats, sleeps, and loves upside down — or of the races of eels that leave European and American rivers to swim thousands of miles to the Bermuda deep, there to breed baby eels that swim all the way back to those same rivers? Such quirks rank as unbelievables because they defy the imagination.

Here, disguised as questions, is your guide to more of the same.

- Are any living creatures jet-propelled?

- Does snake-charming work — or is it just a myth?

- Cockroaches are so horrible that even animals won't eat them. True or false?

- Can fish climb trees?

- Can snakes die of snakebite?

- Which animals use tools?

- Know a creature that travels by sail?

- What's the largest flesh-eating mammal?

- Can snakes fly?

- What's the swiftest animal on four legs. The fastest bird? The speediest creature of all?

- Can anything feed on jellyfish?

- What's a two-headed skink? A Tasmanian devil?

- Can you name the smartest animal — next to man, that is?

- Other than birds and maybe snakes, what animals can fly, or at least glide so well that they simulate flying?

- And here's the final question, a tricky one. It concerns a hunter who walked north 1 mile and without changing course suddenly found himself walking south. Puzzled, he thought it over for exactly 10 minutes, then turned and walked east for

$\frac{1}{2}$ mile, covering the distance in $\frac{1}{2}$ hour. He paused another 10 minutes, looked over his left shoulder and saw a bear. He shot it.

What color was the bear?

85. QUICK MONEY

Tell a friend to curl his hand into a U-shape, as shown. Insert a dollar bill in the opening and make sure his fingers do not touch it. Then challenge him to catch the bill when you let it fall.

Nine times out of ten he can't.

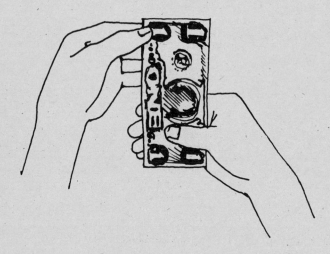

It helps if you keep up a distracting chatter to the effect that now you are about to let the bill fall, that you aren't, that maybe you are, etc.

Hold the bill fairly deep in your friend's hand, so that the top of the bill is near the top of his thumb and forefinger.

If you don't like to play with dollar bills, you can use an ordinary playing card.

86. MAGIC IN MINIATURE

Magic squares have a reputation for occult and mystical properties, weird powers. For centuries they were inscribed on charms and amulets to ward off evil and bring good luck. Hence the name "magic" squares.

Yet the real wonder of these squares has nothing to do with superstition. What makes them unbelievables is the astonishing way in which they illustrate aspects of arithmetic, order, symmetry, number theory, and various branches of higher mathematics. In these small squares, it would seem, is wrapped up all the mathematical magic of the universe.

Square A shows you the first magic square known to have been written down. Part of the so-called Loh River scroll of China, its date is believed to be about 1125.

Remember that a magic square must use consecutive numbers once each to obtain the same sum along rows, files, and diagonals. All right, then. You can easily figure out the Loh River square. Nothing to it.

But as time went on and knowledge of magic squares spread through India and Turkey to Europe, much more complicated ones were devised. They contained fascinating inner patterns and quirks. For example, there were magic squares within magic squares — as in *Square B*.

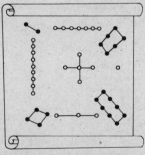

Square A. Loh River
Sum = 15

4	9	8	47	48	49	10
38	19	20	17	34	35	12
39	37	26	27	22	13	11
43	36	21	25	29	14	7
6	18	28	23	24	32	44
5	15	30	33	16	31	45
40	41	42	3	2	1	46

***Square B.* Magic within magic**
Sum of 3 × 3 square = 75
Sum of 5 × 5 square = 125
Sum of 7 × 7 square = 175

One of the many kinds of curiously designed squares is the Indian variety — known also as the diabolical, perfect, or nasik square. It does tricks with the shorter diagonals, bending them or combining them to add up to the magic sum just as the long diagonals do.

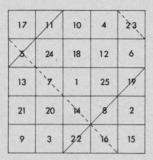

17	11	10	4	23
5	24	18	12	6
13	7	1	25	19
21	20	14	8	2
9	3	22	16	15

Square C. Indian square
Sum = 65

Take *Square C,* for instance. Rows, files and long diagonals add up to 65. But so do any five numbers formed by a shorter diagonal and its complementary opposite diagonal! Two such cases are indicated by the lines in the diagram. 11, 5 and 19, 8, 22 add up to 65. 23 and 5, 7, 14, 16 add up to 65. You can figure out the rest of the cases by yourself.

Note also that the four corner numbers and the center number — 17, 23, 15, 9 and 1 — add up to 65.

French mathematicians developed the construction of magic squares into a high art during the seventeenth century. Then America's own Benjamin Franklin became one of the world's great magic square fans. He created new types of squares with fascinating patterns. *Square D* is a sample.

52	61	4	13	20	29	36	45
14	3	62	51	46	35	30	19
53	60	5	12	21	28	37	44
11	6	59	54	43	38	27	22
55	58	7	10	23	26	39	42
9	8	57	56	41	40	25	24
50	63	2	15	18	31	34	47
16	1	64	49	48	33	32	17

Square D. Franklin square
Sum = 260

Benjamin Franklin dreamed up the "bent" diagonal, as shown in *D-1*, *D-2*, *D-3*, and *D-4*. Along all of these diagonals, *Square D* adds up to 260.

And that's not all. Other symmetrical patterns adding up to 260 were built into the square. Some are shown in *D-5*, *D-6*, *D-7* and *D-8*.

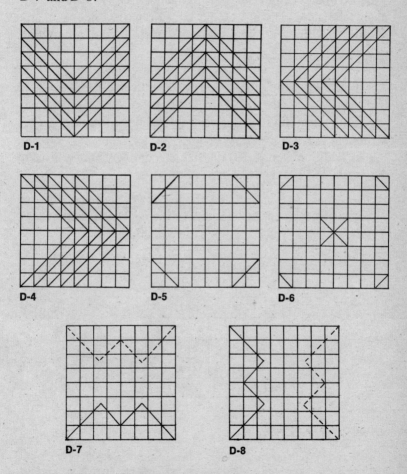

D-1

D-2

D-3

D-4

D-5

D-6

D-7

D-8

(Anywhere on *Square D*, place diagonals like those formed by the solid lines or the broken lines above. The numbers thus covered will add up to 260.)

We see that Benjamin Franklin packed a lot of magic into a small space — rows, files, bent diagonals, and assorted designs. Yet purists would not class the Franklin masterpieces as real magic squares. The long diagonals, alas, fail to total 260!

More than a century later, in England, a Dr. Frierson eliminated the flaw. He also built into Franklin squares many features of Indian squares — as shown in the astounding *Square E*.

• It has Franklin's bent diagonals indicated in *D-1, D-2, D-3,* and *D-4*.

• It has Franklin's symmetrical formations indicated in *D-5* and *D-6*.

• In addition it has certain Indian complementary broken diagonals, indicated in *E-1* and *E-2*.

64	57	4	5	56	49	12	13
3	6	63	58	11	14	55	50
61	60	1	8	53	52	9	16
2	7	62	59	10	15	54	51
48	41	20	21	40	33	28	29
19	22	47	42	27	30	39	34
45	44	17	24	37	36	25	32
18	23	46	43	26	31	38	35

Square E. Frierson's Fancy
Sum = 260

• It has Indian "reflected" diagonals, indicated in *E-3* and *E-4*.

• It has many other startling properties. For instance, it divides into four 4 × 4 squares as shown in *Square E,* each adding up to the same magic sum of 130!

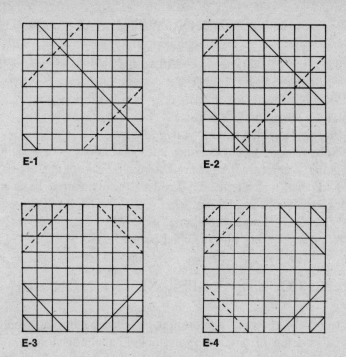

E-1 E-2

E-3 E-4

(Anywhere on *Square E,* place diagonals like those formed by the solid lines or the broken lines above. The numbers thus covered will add up to 260.)

87. ODD MAN OUT

The drill sergeant was nervous. Although he was responsible for less than 500 men, they were to lead the regimental parade and had to make a good showing. He lined them up in ranks of 3 abreast, then 4 abreast, than 5 abreast. Each time there was 1 man left over. So the drill sergeant tried lining them up in ranks of 6. Still there was 1 man left over.

Finally he made one last attempt, lining up the men in ranks of 7. With a sigh of relief, he saw that the ranks came out exactly even. How many men were there?

88. KOOKING WITH GAS

Koko, king of the kooks, konsulted his chief kook about the kooking in the kastle kookerie.

"Koko," kwoth the kook, "only two konditions kan okkur and they are mutually exklusive."

"Kook," kackled Koko, "you're kuckoo."

"Thank you. You see, either a kook is kooking or he is not kooking. Therefore if he is not kooking he is kooking."

King Koko skratched his krown. "You mean if he is not kooking, then he is kooking?"

"Exakly. So kuit komplaining!"

What was wrong with the chief kook's logik?

89. COUNTING OFF AND COUNTING UP

A troop of girl scouts, about to take a bus to a camping ground, have invested in new canteens to hold their drinking water. The scoutmaster, who will have to make do with her old canteen, assigns supervision to the new canteens to whoever is Scout No. 5.

The scouts line up and count off from the left. Scout Jane Smith is No. 5. She makes a face. So the line counts off from the right. Jane is still No. 5. Like it or not, she is stuck with the box of canteens.

She places the box on the back seat of the bus and rides next to it. Noticing that the canteens are stamped with consecutive serial numbers, she amuses herself by adding them up. They total 10026. Announcing that sum, she challenges the other scouts to name the highest serial number.

The girls scoff. Without more information, they say, naming a number would simply be guessing. Are they right? Is it impossible to calculate the highest serial number?

90. FULL EQUALS EMPTY

Dora Dizzy was always swiping cokes. One evening her mother opened the refrigerator, saw that of six bottles she had put in that morning five were empty and the sixth was half-full. She called Dora and gave her a stern lecture about drinking too much coke.

"But a bottle half-full is the same as a bottle half-empty," protested Dora. "I mean $\frac{1}{2}$ equals $\frac{1}{2}$, am I right?"

"I suppose," said her mother.

"Well, if I multiply by 2, I get 1 equals 1 — or a full bottle equals an empty one. Therefore even if I drink a full bottle I'm drinking nothing, so how can you say I drink too much?"

Mrs. Dizzy thought it over. Then she opened the remaining half-bottle and poured the contents on Dora's head. Why?

91. STRETCHING A ROPE

A prisoner of war has stolen a rope 8 feet long. Peering through the bars of his cell, he spots a friendly commando lurking 30 feet below. The daring fellow has sneaked through the enemy lines with a pistol. The prisoner lowers the rope and hoists up the pistol. It enables him to escape the next day.

Unbelievable, you say? Think again. There's an obvious way to make the 8-foot rope reach the pistol.

92. LIGHTNING CALCULATION

Suppose you want to add all the numbers in a consecutive series. The fast way to do it is to add the first and last numbers, divide by 2, and multiply by the number of numbers in the series. For example:

To add the numbers from 5 to 30 —

$$\frac{5 + 30}{2} \times 26 = 455.$$ (Remember that there are 26 numbers, not 25, in this series.)

93. RIDDLE YOU THIS

Word riddles depend on odd coincidences in spelling, double meanings, twists of thought, and the like, all so surprising that a good riddle, in a sense, may be classed as an unbelievable.

Here are some samples that have been around since the beginning of the nineteenth century and earlier. They still make people laugh, and you can believe that — for modern comedians often rely on these very riddles or variations of them.

Why is a thinking man like a mirror?

He reflects.

What is it that if you name, you break?

Silence.

Why is a room crowded with married folks the same as an empty room?

There's not a single person in it.

In which month do ladies talk least?

February — it's the shortest.

What word, when you add a syllable to it, becomes shorter?

Short.

What most resembles a dog in a hole?

A dog out of a hole.

How many sides are there to a baseball?

Inside and outside.

Why do we go to school?

The school won't come to us.

One prominent pair of comedians provoked gales of laughter with a routine based on the ancient riddle:

Why do white sheep eat more than black sheep?

There are more white sheep.

Sometimes the comics make "switches" in order to keep the riddles fresh. For example, in the 1800's this riddle was popular:

When Napoleon landed on St. Helena, on what did he stand?

On his feet.

Today the riddle is worded, "When Candidate Blank debates international policy, where does he stand?" And sometimes the answer is switched from "on his feet" to "on his head."

Try amusing your friends with these riddles. When and if they start to go stale, perhaps you can change them slightly to freshen them or even make up new ones — always bearing in mind this last riddle:

Why is a riddle like a railroad car?

Both can be switched.

94. COUNTING THE COPS

Four perfectly straight avenues, running through a park, cross each other at various points. Motor traffic is so heavy that the authorities decide to put on enough extra police to post one at each crossing for seven hours every weekday. At most, how many additional policemen must be hired — assuming none ever gets sick or goes on vacation?

Believe it or not, the answer is not four.

95. DOT IN A CIRCLE

You don't have to believe this, either. But the fact is that without lifting your pencil from the paper, you can draw the figure shown:

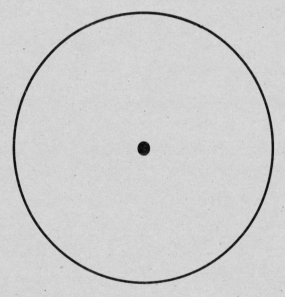

Don't bother trying to draw neatly or accurately; a rough circle and a rough dot will do. Just make sure your pencil point touches the paper at all times.

96. PLAYING SQUARE WITH YOURSELF

You wouldn't believe how many parts a square can be divided into by four straight lines. What's your guess?

97. A FLOCK OF FEET

In a Florida bird sanctuary live a number of herons. They roost in a pool or in trees. Of those roosting in the pool, some stand on one foot. Half the rest roost in trees.

When all the herons are roosting, how many feet are in the pool?

98. THE TERRIBLE TEN

Take nine toothpicks and with them make three triangular figures, as shown.

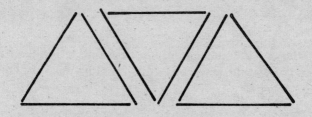

Now out of the three figures, form ten — permitting no toothpick to rest atop another.

ANSWER SECTION

2. SEE? — NO HANDS!

The explanation for this phenomenon is based on Bernoulli's principle, which states that when air is in rapid motion, there is an increase of pressure as the velocity of the air decreases and a decrease of pressure as the velocity increases. Since the air is rushing out quickly in both directions between the loose playing card and the small piece of glued cardboard, pressure decreases above the card. Thus the pressure of air from the bottom holds the card to the spool.

3. AMAZING COLOR WHEEL

This visual effect is difficult to understand. The eye tends to move from left to right in a straight line; but when that line is cut off by the black half-circle and caught up by the curvature, the light is bent and color results.

4. MYSTERY MAN

He is the weatherman, whose predictions are followed by millions daily in the newspapers and on radio and TV. Do you know his name?

5. GOING TWO WAYS AT ONCE

To explain this phenomenon, consider a train wheel. As you know, it has a flange or rim, so that part of the wheel is below the rail, as shown in the figure. Now it is clear that, as the section of the wheel in contact with the rail is rotating rapidly, the section below the rail is rotating just as rapidly in the opposite direction. Since this is true for every wheel on the entire train, including the engine, you can see that part of the forward-moving train is actually and always moving backward.

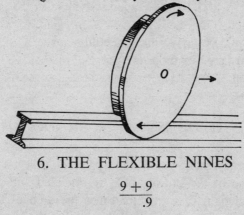

6. THE FLEXIBLE NINES

$$\frac{9+9}{.9}$$

7. SOME PILE!

It would take approximately five thousand pages the thickness of this one to make a pile one foot high, or 26,400,000 pages to make a pile a mile high. Fifty-three cuttings of a piece of paper the thickness of this page would be calculated as two raised to the fifty-third power, or nine billion million sheets. Figuring twenty-six million sheets to the mile, the pile would be approximately 350 million miles high. The area of this page is about thirty-seven and a half square inches, and nine million billion times this would produce 290 million billion square inches. Figuring four billion square inches to the square mile, the area of the original sheet of paper would have to be seventy million square miles — or approximately twenty-three times the area of the United States!

10. GUESS WHAT?

The mysterious object is *fire*.

11. A BILLION — MORE OR LESS

a. You would be forty-nine years old.
b. It would take two thousand years.

12. HYDROSTATIC PARADOX

It is a well-known principle, stated by Pascal, that the pressure on the surface of the bottom of a vessel filled with water is equal to the height of the water times the area of the base. Since the height of the water and the area of the base are the same for A and B, the pressure will be the same for both vessels — regardless of their shape.

15. PASSING A SOLID THROUGH AN IRON GRILLE

Ice melts under pressure. For example, when you ice-skate, your weight melts the ice directly under the blade of the skate, and you go sliding along on a thin film of water. The instant your skate leaves this spot, the water freezes again, just as though nothing had happened. In the same way, the pressure of the hundred-pound cake of ice on the wires of the grille melts the ice at that point, and the huge mass gradually sinks lower and lower until it goes right through the grille, without leaving a mark.

16. INCREDIBLE BUT TRUE

The cardboard is prevented from falling off the glass because of atmospheric pressure, which is almost fifteen pounds per square inch. This means that the air presses up against the bottom of the cardboard with a force of about forty pounds, which is much more than the weight of the water in the glass.

18. GYROGEOMETRY

AB is the same length as the radius, or 8.2 feet, since the diagonals of the rectangle are equal.

19. THE DISAPPEARING DOLLAR

The clerk gave back five dollars and kept twenty-five dollars. The boy gave each man one dollar and kept two dollars. Each man paid nine dollars, less two dollars for the boy, making a total of twenty-five dollars.

20. CANNON-BALL CONUNDRUM

Gravity acts independently of horizontal motion. At the end of the first second, both cannon balls will be sixteen feet lower than when they started. At the end of the second second, they will both be sixty-four feet lower. So no matter how far out the first ball is shot, it will always be as far from the horizontal as the dropped ball, and hence both balls will hit the ground at the same time.

22. REVOLUTIONARY PROBLEM

As it rotates, the little wheel is also *sliding*. But this sliding action is so evenly distributed that it is not noticed.

23. FOUR-IN-ONE

Julian married the mother of his father's second wife, and they had a son. His stepmother also had a son. Julian is therefore the father of his stepmother's nephew, the husband of his father's mother-in-law, and the father-in-law of his stepmother. He is also his own grandfather.

24. MYSTERIOUS TRIANGLE

Of course, the idea that 4 equals 2 is absurd, yet this would seem to be the case if we increased the number of triangles to infinity. But since infinity can never be reached, the sum total of the sides of the millions of triangles on the base line will still be four inches. This is the same principle as cutting a line in half indefinitely: There will always be a half remaining, no matter how infinitesimally small that half may be.

28. FIVE DAYS IN SPACE

The fallacy here is that we think of the astronaut as being on the *earth*, whereas actually he was not. The earth rotates once in twenty-four hours; consequently the position of the sun on the earth is different for different localities, and so is the time of day. That is why we have time zones on earth.

For an astronaut traveling several hundred miles above the earth, there is no such thing as day and night. The sky is inky black, and the sun neither rises nor sets. Therefore his only measure of time is his earthly timepiece. Lieutenant Bykovsky knew that the hour hand of his watch had made ten complete revolutions while he was up in space.

29. SOMETHING TO EXCLAIM ABOUT

In mathematics, an exclamation point is used, not as punctuation, but to denote a process. Whenever you see a number followed by an exclamation mark, it means *factorial* — the product of all numbers from 1 to the given number. For example, $3! = 1 \times 2 \times 3$, or 6. $7! = 1 \times 2 \times 3 \times 4 \times 5 \times 6 \times 7$, or 5,040. So now you can see why 20! is such an enormously high number.

30. ALWAYS ROOM FOR ONE MORE

Surface tension allows the water to expand above the rim like a rubber sheet, thus making room for the tiny amount of water displaced by each pin. Of course, if you keep adding pins there will come a time when water will start to drip over imperceptibly.

32. PROVING THE IMPOSSIBLE

The geometry is correct, but the construction is faulty. Point O will fall much farther down than shown, and therefore triangles ACO and B'DO will not be equal.

33. BOILING WATER IN A PAPER CUP

The water in the cup keeps the cup cool, thus preventing the flame from reaching the kindling temperature necessary to set the paper on fire.

36. STICK 'EM UP WITHOUT STICKUM

A playing card will stick to the wall if you hold it in your hand and rub your feet along the carpet slowly, and then hit the card sharply against the wall. Static electricity does the rest.

38. EVERY TRIANGLE IS ISOSCELES

If this were true, it would upset our geometric concepts. The fallacy is hidden in the diagram. Note that point O lies *outside* of the triangle, as does perpendicular OD or OE — but not both. If we draw the diagram correctly, so that O and both perpendiculars fall inside the triangle, then this preposterous "theorem" cannot be proved and the laws of geometry are still valid.

39. GETTING OVER THE HUMP

If the ground were absolutely flat, the pipe would rise toward the middle in two straight lines, or in an arc so gentle as to be the equivalent of two straight lines. An imaginary vertical line in the middle would therefore, in effect, complete two right-angle triangles, as shown in the diagram (exaggerated). The hypotenuse would be one-half mile or 2,640 feet. The base would be one-half 5,279 feet or $2,639\frac{1}{2}$ feet. Hypotenuse squared minus the base squared gives the height of the vertical line squared. Unsquaring the latter, you find the height of the hump to be between 51 and 52 feet.

40. MONKEY BUSINESS

The weight will go up.

41. NOW YOU SEE IT — NOW YOU DON'T

You cannot see the coin because of refraction. The water refracts the light so much that the angle is beyond what is known as the critical angle, and as you look through it the glass becomes a mirror. You can get the same effect by holding a glass of water above your eye level and noting the bottom surface of the water. It will be a mirror.

42. THREE QUERIES

a. Since ship B is on the horizon, it can be only fifteen miles away, because the horizon is always the same distance from the observer, no matter which direction he faces or how far off the object.

b. If you examine the diagram carefully, you will note that the ground behind pole B slopes away from the sun. The slope elongates the shadow.

c. Place the mirrors so that they form a right angle, as shown.

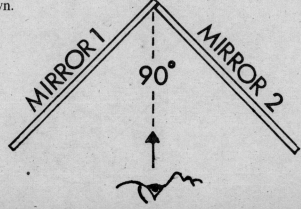

43. MY GRANDSON IS OLDER THAN I AM

This statement is not as preposterous as it seems at first glance when you realize that it is based on the *binary system,* instead of the more common decimal system. The decimal system has ten digits, from 0 through 9, whereas the binary system has only two: 0 and 1. In the binary system, 110 is equivalent to 4 in the decimal system, 1,110 is 14, and 10,101 is 21. Translating, then, from the binary to the decimal system, the statement now reads: "My grandson has just turned four years old. I have hopes that in ten years he will be entering high school, and that by the time he is twenty-one he will be finishing college."

48. TRISECTING AN ANGLE WITH RULER AND COMPASS

The proof of this trisection is extremely simple. Since AB equals BC, ABC is isosceles and 0 equals angle BCA. But angle DBC is twice angle 0. Now simply draw a line through C parallel to line AD. The smaller angle equals 0 and the larger angle equals angle DBC. But angle DBC equals twice angle 0, consequently angle 0 equals two times 0 plus angle 0, or three times angle 0.

49. THE CRESCENT AND THE CROSS

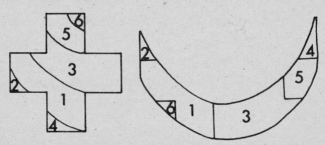

50. ON THE GO

Joe Doaks is an elevator operator in the Empire State Building in New York City — the tallest building in the world.

53. FALL SAFE

Few people realize that the *main* roof of the Empire State Building is only four stories high. So it is possible to jump off this roof and land on a mat or other soft covering without serious injury.

55. NOT A SHADE OF DIFFERENCE

The size of a shadow cast by an object increases as the distance of the object from its source of light — in this case the sun. But since the sun is ninety-three million miles away, a difference of four hundred and fifty feet — the difference between the distances of the two planes from the ground — is negligible, so both shadows appear to be the same size.

56. MAGNETIC HILL

It is an optical illusion. The conformation of the surrounding countryside makes the slope appear to run in the opposite direction from what it actually does. Even the little brook that trickles by the roadside appears to flow uphill.

59. DOUBLE DILEMMA

The man told the king's sons to change horses and race to town!

60. CALLING ALL COMMAS!

1. Not "and," I said, but "or."
2. That that is, is; that that is not, is not.
3. Whereas in the quiz Jones had had "had," Smith had had "had had." Had "had had" had the examiner's approval, Smith would have passed.

64. FUN WITH FIGURES

a. The correct answer is 206.25. The other answer is wrong because the fractions have been multiplied *twice*.

b. The fallacy lies in the fact that a-b = 0, and it is mathematically impossible to divide by 0.

c. Joan is one year old, John is two hours old, and Jane is only one hour old!

66. UNBELIEVABLE GEOGRAPHY

At the junction of Utah, Colorado, New Mexico, and Arizona — the only four states that touch each other.

67. SHORTHAND — OR IS IT LONGHAND?

a. Write down 123 − 45 − 67 + 89. Work it out, and you'll see that in effect you wrote down 100.

b. $99 \frac{99}{99}$, $88 \frac{88}{88}$, $77 \frac{77}{77}$.

69. GEOGRAPHY JAMBOREE

a. Nothing. Madrid is approximately due west of New York City.

b. He is right.

c. Pittsburgh lies practically due north of the Panama Canal.

d. 1-F; 2-T; 3-F (Alaska is more than twice as large as Texas); 4-F (Michigan does); 5-T; 6-T; 7-T; 8-T; 9-T; 10-T (Kansas City lies slightly east); 11-F; 12-F; 13-F; 14-F; 15-T; 16-F; 17-T; 18-T.

70. INFLATION OR DEFLATION

Yes, the square roots of equal numbers are equal. But 25 and $\frac{1}{4}$ are not equal numbers. They only read as if they were because the words "cents" and "dollar" are inserted.

Put another way, 25 cents as a number would read .25 and $\frac{1}{4}$ dollar as a number would read .25. Now the numbers are seen to be equal — and their respective square roots (.5) are equal.

71. PUZZLE OF THE POOL

The area of the opening in the 6-inch pipe would be larger than the combined areas of the openings in the two 3-inch pipes. Therefore the 6-inch pipe would fill the pool faster. (It is not necessary to calculate the cubic capacity of the pipes.)

72. TWO SHAPES FOR ONE

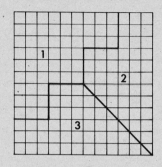

74. BY SPECIAL ARRANGEMENT

Sam packed the pole diagonally into a shallow crate 3 feet wide by 6½ feet long.

75. UNBELIEVABLY TRIANGULAR

The five-point star drawn with five straight lines creates ten triangles as follows:

There are five overlapping triangles in the star — 1,3, 10; 2,5,9; 4,1,8; 2,4,6; 5,7,3.

And there are five nonoverlapping triangles in the star — 1,7,6; 2,7,8; 3,9,8; 4,10,9; 5,6,10.

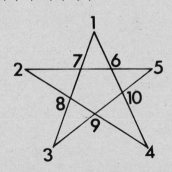

76. DRAMA IN ANCIENT ROME

Brutus is wrong, from Cassius' point of view. Turn this book upside down and you'll see that to Cassius the equation looks like this:

$$X = I + IX$$

78. GUESSING ODD OR EVEN

Sue asked that Gilbert double his number and Billy triple his, then add the results.

She knew that if the sum were even, Gilbert had chosen the odd number — therefore Billy had chosen the even number.

She knew that if the sum were odd, Gilbert had chosen the even number — therefore Billy had chosen the odd number.

79. HOW FOXY CAN YOU GET

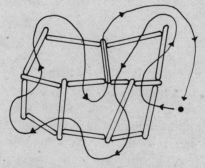

83. FREAKS OF PHYSICS

• The ice displaces an amount of water greater than the amount it makes when it melts. Therefore the displaced water leaves plenty of room for the melting water.

• Salt melts ice by transferring heat to it. When the ice is packed around ice cream and melted by salt, the melting also draws heat from the ice cream — thus freezing it.

• When water starts to freeze, it expands for a while before it begins to contract, thus violating a practically universal law of nature — and thus bursting the pipe.

• The specific gravity of skim milk is greater than that of cream.

• Some of the alcohol dissolves in the water; the alcohol molecules tend to permeate the water molecules.

• This is difficult to picture. But you'll admit that after the two transfers, a definite quantity of water has been removed from the water gallon. Therefore it must have been replaced by an equal quantity of alcohol. And whatever quantity of alcohol has been removed from the alcohol gallon must have been replaced by an equal amount of water.

84. ASK MOTHER NATURE

• Octopuses and squid both can swim by sucking in water and squirting it out in a jet.

• There is some question about whether snakes can hear in the same sense that humans do. But snakes do react to vibrations like those set in motion by a footfall or a musical instrument. It is substantiated that they will grow taut and hypnotized in response to certain notes of, say, a flute or a piano — or even the sounds of a radio. In such a state the snake may "dance" — that is, sway — as the snake-charmer plays his instrument. Some maintain, however, that the response is not to the notes but to the swaying of the snake-charmer on whom the snake's attention is fixed.

• Cockroaches are a diet prized by that creature of many colors, the chameleon.

• Certain gurnards, gobies, and other species, in search of molluscs and grubs, occasionally will climb root extensions and low limbs dipping into the water.

• Rattlers can. A rattlesnake bitten by another during a fight may die in a few hours.

• There are cases, it is said, of primates using one banana to probe for another banana. But a finch of the Galapagos Islands is the only authenticated tool user. Grasping a thorn or twig in its beak, it will poke the tool into holes in tree limbs to dislodge bugs and grubs.

• Portuguese men-of-war and certain similar sea creatures consist of colonies of polyps, each with a specialized function such as stinging, gathering, eating etc. One polyp erects itself into a definite sail that catches the wind and keeps the beastie moving.

• The killer whale, up to 30 feet long, eats its brother whales and anything else it can sink its teeth into. The Alaskan brown bear, weighing half a ton or more, is the largest of the land carnivores.

• In Malaysia lives a 2-foot-long variety of snake that can stretch its skin into a kind of flying wing. It soars through the air from tree to tree, hunting lizards.

• The cheetah runs fastest, exceeding 70 miles per hour for short distances. Varieties of the swift in America, Asia, and Australia reach speeds of 200 to 250 miles per hour. But a kind of deerfly (*Cephenomia*) takes the prize. It travels so fast that it has never been accurately timed. Expert estimates, however, place its flying speed at more than 500 miles per hour and perhaps as high as 818 miles per hour.

• Jellyfish seem to consist either of globs of nothing or tangles of stinging tentacles. Yet they are considered tidbits by sea-going birds like the stormy petrel and the albatross.

• A skink is a lizard, ranging from a couple of inches to perhaps a foot in length, and in the United States found as far north as New England. Scales on the tail of one variety are arranged in the form of a second head, hence the name "two-headed skink."

• A Tasmanian devil is doglike marsupial found only in — you guessed it — Tasmania. Fierce in the wild, it is nevertheless easily tamed.

• There is the flying gurnard, a variety of the fish previously mentioned, whose fins can extend like wings. Whether it actually soars is not certain. But consider the flying lizard of the East Indies, which can soar from one tree to another — maybe to escape the flying snake previously mentioned. There is also the bat, a mammal able to outfly many a bird. And there are the flying fox, the flying squirrel, the flying fish; all can leap, soar, or glide in a fair approximation of flight. Nor should we forget the flying phalanger of Australasia, a beastie two or three feet long, equipped with folds of skin that enable it to make parachute jumps.

• Obviously the hunter was somewhere near the North Pole, for he was able to travel north and then south without turning or otherwise changing course. So his bear had to be a polar bear, and therefore white.

87. ODD MAN OUT

There were 301 men, making 43 ranks of 7 men each.

88. KOOKING WITH GAS

A vital negative was omitted. The chief kook should have said, "Therefore if he is *not* not kooking he is kooking."

89. COUNTING OFF AND COUNTING UP

Since Jane is No. 5 whether the line counts off from left or right, there must be 9 scouts. Since there are 9 scouts, there must be 9 canteens. Since they bear numbers that add up to 10026, that number divided by 9 will give the average of the serial numbers, or 1114. Since the 9 serial numbers run consecutively, there must be four consecutively lower and four consecutively higher than the average.

Therefore the serial numbers must be 1110, 1111, 1112, 1113, 1114, 1115, 1116, 1117 — and the highest, 1118.

90. FULL EQUALS EMPTY

Mrs. Dizzy was in a tizzy because Dora's logic was ridiculous. True, equals multiplied by the same number are equal. So if both sides are multiplied by 2, $\frac{1}{2} = \frac{1}{2}$ becomes $1 = 1$. But that refers to bottles, not the contents of same. Regarding the coke within the bottles, Dora was claiming that $1 = 0$ — an absurdity.

91. STRETCHING A ROPE

The prisoner unraveled the rope into its three main strands and tied them end to end, making a new rope nearly 24 feet long. Even if the commando were only 5 feet tall, he could still reach high enough to tie the pistol to the end of the elongated rope.

94. COUNTING THE COPS

At first glance the greatest number of crossings four straight avenues can make is four, as shown in Diagram A. But actually four straight avenues can make six crossings, as shown in Diagram B. So six additional policemen would have to be hired.

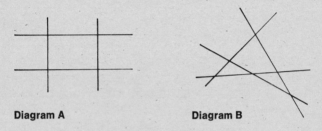

Diagram A   **Diagram B**

95. DOT IN A CIRCLE

Fold a corner of the paper onto itself. Make a dot on the paper, then push the pencil along the folded-over corner as shown in *Figure 1*. Finally, push the pencil off the corner, fold the corner back out of the way, and draw your circle as in *Figure 2*.

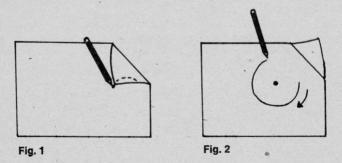

Fig. 1   **Fig. 2**

96. PLAYING SQUARE WITH YOURSELF

Most persons place the four lines as in *Figures A, B,* or *C,* yielding 8 parts. Some place the lines as in *Figure D,* yielding 9 parts. But an arrangement like that in *Figure E* yields 11 parts.

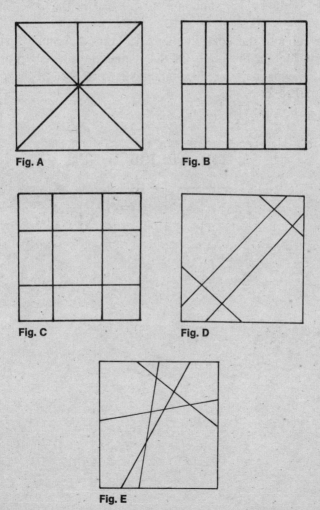

Fig. A

Fig. B

Fig. C

Fig. D

Fig. E

97. A FLOCK OF FEET

As many feet as there are cranes! Unbelievable, you say? Here's proof.

Suppose the flock numbers 60 cranes. Assume 30 stand on one foot in the pool. Of the remaining 30, half roost in trees, leaving half, or 15, standing on *two* feet in the pool. $30 + (15 \times 2) = 60$.

Or suppose the flock numbers 45 cranes. Assume 5 stand on one foot in the pool. Of the remaining 40, half roost in trees, leaving half, or 20, standing on two feet in the pool. $5 + (20 \times 2) = 45$.

98. THE TERRIBLE TEN

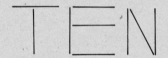